D1711937

Spain

Spain has undergone great political change this century, living through civil war and an oppressive dictatorship under General Franco. It is only since his death in 1975, when King Juan Carlos came to power, that a more democratic form of government has been established. However, internal political problems remain. Feelings run high over the fight for independence from central government by the people of various regions, notably the Basque country.

Many people have come to know Spain through the popularity of its coastal towns and villages as vacation resorts. Since the 1960s, the tourist trade has grown to become one of Spain's major industries. The influx of foreign tourists has also served to help relax the powerful influence exercised by the Catholic Church, and modernize some of the attitudes enforced by an oppressive regime.

In *We Live in Spain*, a cross-section of the Spanish people tell you what their life is like – life in the city, on the coast, in the mountains, in the countryside.

The author, Richard Bristow, has traveled all over Spain. He now lives in Barcelona, where he is a freelance journalist and photographer.

ATLANTIC OCEAN

FRANCE

GALICIA

ASTURIAS

• Bilbao

BASQUE PROVINCES

NAVARRA

• Pamplona

Pyrenees

LEON

River Duero

CASTILLA LA VIEJA

• Salamanca

River Ebro

• Zaragoza

Gerona

Segovia

PORTUGAL

CATALUÑA

• Barcelona

Madrid

River Tajo

CASTILLA LA NUEVA

River Guadiana

ESTREMADURA

VALENCIA

MALLORCA

ME

Valencia

Cordoba

Sevilla

River Guadalquivir

MURCIA

IBIZA

ANDALUCIA

Alicante

Granada

Sierra Nevada

Cartagena

Malaga

Torremolinos

MEDITERRANEAN SEA

we live in
SPAIN

Richard Bristow

A Living Here Book

The Bookwright Press
New York · 1904

Living Here

First published in the United States in 1984 by
The Bookwright Press, 387 Park Avenue South,
New York NY 10016

First published in 1982 by
Wayland (Publishers) Limited, England

© Copyright 1982 Wayland (Publishers) Ltd.

ISBN: 0−531−04780−6

Library of Congress Catalog Card Number: 83−72806

Printed by G. Canale & C.S.p.A., Turin, Italy

Contents

"I'm there to represent the people"

Amadeo Gallart, 45, is a trader in wines and liquor in Seu d'Urgel in Lerida. In 1979 he was elected mayor of the town, which is in Cataluña (Catalonia). He feels that the municipal government is the backbone of democracy.

I was elected mayor of Seu d'Urgel in 1979, when we had the first democratic elections since the Civil War. Seu d'Urgel is a town of about 10,000 inhabitants. It is the market town for the area. Being mayor in a town like mine is very different from being mayor in a large town or city. In a city, it's a full-time job and you get paid accordingly, but here I am not paid at all for my work as mayor. So I have to split my time between being mayor and earning a living by

This is the Town Hall, where I hope the people of Seu d'Urgel will gain the confidence to bring their problems.

working as a trader in wines and liquor.

I'm a member of the *Partit Socialista Unificat de Cataluña*, which is the Catalan equivalent of the Spanish Communist Party. I'm in favor of all councilors belonging to a political party, because it means that they are represented in the central parliament in Madrid. But, at a local level, I think it is good for all the left-wing and progressive parties to join forces, in order to bring about the reforms that this country needs.

On an average, my work as mayor occupies about thirty hours a week. At least once each week, the town council (twelve councilors and myself) meets to discuss problems.

One of our main problems is town planning. In recent years there has been a tremendous increase in new buildings in the town, without any proper planning. Now we're trying to clear up the muddle and create a town which is more pleasant to live in – conserving and renovating beautiful old buildings and reserving land for parks, schools, or other facilities.

At the moment we're still very limited in what we can do, because the laws regarding the legal and financial powers of municipal councils have not been changed since General Franco was in power. In those days, mayors were responsible to the civil governors of the province. But now we have to answer to the people of our town for our actions, because they elected us. The problem is that the purse strings are still controlled by the government in Madrid and they give us virtually no money to spend on building or social services. In this way, we aren't really independent as a council.

The image of the mayor who is the richest or most important man in town is no longer true. The 1979 elections brought in a new class of people. In general, local government positions in Spain are now filled by ordinary working people, most of whom have left-wing beliefs.

As mayor, I have to take part in the town's fiesta, which is a bit like a carnival. I enjoy this very much. Here, and in most of Cataluña (Catalonia), huge models of giants are a traditional part of the celebrations – the children love them. Every town and village in Spain has its own *fiesta*, which usually takes place on the day dedicated to its patron saint.

Perhaps my greatest problem (and that of any person in a position of authority in Spain) is to overcome the general lack of confidence people have in government institutions. People don't expect the Town Hall to be able to solve their problems, or in fact to help them in any way at all. It is very difficult to convince people that things have changed and that I'm here to represent them, not just to speak for the central government.

This is a fundamental problem which must be overcome – as I feel that the municipal government is the backbone of democracy.

All children love the giants, which are a traditional part of our town's fiesta.

"The Spanish like to eat well"

Juan José Medina, 32, has traveled all over Spain working in the kitchens of many hotels and restaurants, first as kitchen boy – later as chef. He now owns a restaurant in Bilbao, which he runs with his wife.

I own a small restaurant in Bilbao. I run it with my wife Mercedes – I do the cooking, she helps out with the serving and looks after the cash register. Two boys work for us as waiter and barman and we run the place like a family business. This is fairly typical these days, as wages have gone up so much that it's almost impossible to afford to employ a big staff, unless you operate on a very large scale and can be sure of a lot of customers every day.

I was born in Burgos, but when I was seventeen I decided to become a chef, so I left school and started traveling around Spain, working in hotels and restaurants. I stayed in each place for about six months – just long enough to learn how to make the dishes typical of each region. In this way I worked my way up from kitchen helper to chef.

I always see to the cooking myself.

A *shellfish* paella – *one of the most well-known Spanish dishes, which is always popular with my customers.*

I was twenty-eight when I decided to open my own restaurant, and I chose Bilbao because it's a city which is famous for its food. Each day I prepare a small menu of a few special dishes, so I don't have to keep big stocks of frozen foods. I go to the market every morning at 6 a.m. to buy the food, choosing the vegetables and meats that are best quality and value on that particular day. I decide how to cook them afterwards.

A typical menu might offer *gazpacho andaluz* (a cold soup made with garlic, onions, tomatoes, peppers and bread-crumbs) or cured ham with melon to start. It may be followed by mussels, giant prawns, or squid cooked in its own ink. The main dish may be *paella valenciana* (a rice-based dish containing a variety of fish and meat, such as shellfish, octopus, mussels, chicken and rabbit), or it may be roast suckling pig (typical of Segovia), or roast lamb. I have lamb sent from Burgos by an uncle who is a butcher. Burgos is famous for its lamb. Another day the main dishes could well be fish, because around here we can buy very good fish straight off the boats as they come in.

The price I charge for a meal like this is obviously not that cheap. You can eat in many *restaurantes caseros* (home-cooking restaurants) for perhaps 200 – 300 pesetas ($1.50 – $2.25), including wine and dessert. My menu costs 1,200 pesetas (almost $9.00) and I don't include the price of wine.

In Bilbao, there are gastronomical clubs for people interested in food. The club house is usually an apartment that has a very well-equipped kitchen. There is also a dining area. The members (usually men) are enthusiastic about cooking and they organize dinner parties at the clubs, bringing along their own food and doing all the cooking themselves.

I would say that as a race, the Spanish are especially interested in eating well.

"Nobody was killed last year"

Enrique Molina, 47, was born in Granada and began to learn bullfighting when he was 11. He became a *matador* when he was 23, and has fought in all the important bullrings in Spain. At present he lives in Sevilla.

I was born in Alhama in the province of Granada. My interest in bullfighting was sparked off by listening to my parents discussing bullfights. I was eleven when I saw my first bullfight and decided that I just had to become a *matador*. I entered a competition for budding *matadors* – and won it. My prize was the opportunity to go once a week to the bullring in Malaga and receive lessons from an instructor. Apart from that I spent hours on end practicing with a friend of mine. He would charge at me with a pair of horns mounted on a sort of wheelbarrow, while I tried to imitate the *matadors* I'd seen in the bullring the previous Sunday.

When I was twelve I started practicing with two-year-old bulls weighing about 180 kilos (400lb). These bullfights took place in small bullrings and were a good way of gaining some experience. About a year later, when I was thirteen, I made my début in Valencia as a *novillero* (novice

The picador *weakens the bull's neck with a pike in the first* tercio.

bullfighter) in a real bullfight, fighting a young bull of about 250 kilos (550lb).

Although I started bullfighting very early, it took me ten years of hard work to become a *matador*. During this time I traveled all over Spain and fought in all the most important bullrings. Lots of experience is essential if you want to stay alive, which is why I was twenty-three by the time I became a *matador*. That is also why they call a *matador* "Maestro."

Bullfighting originated in Arabia, started by noblemen who would fight bulls with a lance on horseback, in order to impress the ladies. Over the centuries things have changed considerably and these days the only person who rides a horse is the *picador*. He enters the bullring in the first *tercio* (third) of the fight and sticks a pike, a lance, into the bull's neck. The second *tercio* is called *banderrillas*. Here a man on foot (and with no protection) sticks two *banderillas*, which are decorated barbed darts, into the bull. The third *tercio* is *la muerte* (the death) and this is where the *matador* shows his art with the cape. By now the bull is extremely angry at having things stuck into him — and is ready to kill. The *matador* stands still and goads the bull into charging at him by flapping the red cape. The bull is fooled into running at the cape instead of the *matador*, who sidesteps at the last minute. These passes with the cape go on until the bull begins to tire and the *matador* considers that it is time for the final *estocada* (sword-thrust). This is the *matador's* bravest moment. To kill the bull he must go and lean over its horns in order to plunge the sword into the back of its neck.

Many serious wounds are caused by being caught by the bull's horns. I have been lucky. Although I've been caught several times, my injuries have not been

The last tercio, *when the* matador *shows his skill with the cape.*

too bad. Thanks to specialized surgery and antibiotics, the death rate of bullfighters has dropped considerably. In fact, the Bullfighters' Association erected a monument to Dr. Alexander Fleming, who discovered the antibiotic penicillin. Last year no one was killed and the year before only one bullfighter died.

These days, bullfighting isn't so popular as it was. Everyone talks about soccer instead. Apart from that, many people prefer to spend their free time going off to the country or to the beach.

Years ago, becoming a *matador* was a way of escaping from poverty and becoming famous. Nowadays, life is different. Boys think about studying for a career rather than risking their lives in front of a bull.

"Real flamenco is a lament"

Flora Callado Caparros is 24 and teaches flamenco dancing to children. She was a professional dancer for thirteen years, gaining her first dancing contract at the age of 10. She lives in Teruel.

I was born in Teruel but my parents and their families come from Andalucia. I always liked dancing and when I was seven my parents began sending me to a flamenco dancing school three times a week. After about four months the teacher said that I had a real talent. She recommended that I should take ballet classes

This is the traditional ruffled dress worn by flamenco dancers.

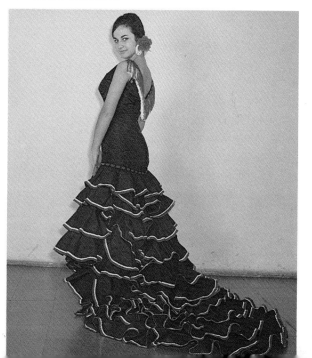

too, so that I would have a good basic knowledge of the classical dance movements. So I attended both ballet and flamenco classes, each for three hours a week.

I did my first show when I was eight and when I was ten I got my first contract to dance in a *Sala de fiestas*. I was paid 50 pesetas (37 cents) per show. I kept on with my dancing classes because you need to do a lot of training and practice in order to dance flamenco well. As most of my shows were in the evening, I was able to combine this work with my dancing classes and school.

When I was sixteen I started going on tours with a dance company. Although I performed all types of folk dances, my main act was a flamenco dance, accompanied by a singer and a guitarist. In my opinion, no other musical instrument can "speak" like the guitar. For a performance of flamenco to be complete, there should be a singer who explains the movements of the dancer through song, and a guitarist who accompanies both the singer and the dancer.

For me, flamenco is a ritual. I think in many ways it is similar to traditional blues music, in this sense: you are able to understand the feelings behind the music and the song without necessarily understanding the words.

There are various themes in flamenco, and the one I like best is the *solea*, which is generally considered to be the original basic theme. The other themes are really just variations on it. The *solea* tells the story of very poor people – usually a family. All the family goes out to do back-breaking work in the fields, to try to scrape a living from the soil. Meanwhile, the mother is at home trying to do miracles with the little she has to feed her family. Her life is a mixture of misery, hardship, and suffering. But despite everything she must always be cheerful, smiling, and grateful to God or nature for having provided something for her family.

Very often it is said that to see real flamenco one has to see it danced by gypsies, but true flamenco has very little to do with gypsies. The gypsy flamenco is colorful, spontaneous and *alegre* (happy). But traditional flamenco is something very different – it is certainly not *alegre*. I would describe it as a lament which reflects the suffering and hardship of poor people. It is not spontaneous either. To sing or dance flamenco requires hours of rehearsals. By this I don't mean to say that gypsy flamenco is not good – it is, but it's just not real flamenco.

I gave up dancing in shows a year ago, as it was very difficult to combine them with my family life. Now I teach flamenco classes for children in the afternoons instead. All the children love dancing and they really enjoy playing the *castañuelas* (castanets) and stamping their feet. I don't think any of them are dedicated enough to take up professional dancing. It'll just be a hobby for them.

In my classes, the children really enjoy playing the castanets.

"Not enough hospitals for everyone"

Maria Torrens, 26, is a nurse in the infants' ward of a state hospital in Valencia. Her parents would not allow her to leave home earlier to study to be a veterinarian. She's only now moving out to her own apartment.

I finished my high-school education at sixteen. I wanted to study to be a vet. But the only two universities that offer the course are in Madrid and Zaragoza, and my parents would not allow me to leave home. So I decided to study to be a nurse or *Asistenta Técnica Sanitaria*, as it is called here. The course took three years and when I qualified I got a job in one of the hospitals in Valencia. I work in an infants' ward (children up to two years old). My duty hours are very long. I work twelve hours at a stretch. But I'm only on duty every other day and so I have quite a bit of free time – which makes up for a lot.

In Spain we have a lot of private clinics, which are very expensive. People tend to take out private insurance to cover the cost of any medical treatment they might need, including specialists' fees and hospital treatment. There is, of course, national health insurance here which provides good, well-equipped state hospitals, but there just aren't enough hospitals for everyone. If you want to see a doctor, you either have to go to a *centro ambulatorio* (a sort of small medical center) or to a hospital. Usually there is a long line and you have to wait for hours. We don't have family doctors' practices provided by the health service except in rural areas, where there are no other centers. Elsewhere, there are only private doctors, who are expensive. The same applies to dentists. Many parts of Spain are very isolated and there are not many doctors who want to go and work there. This is partly because there are so few facilities and partly because they can earn a better living in one of the big towns or cities.

If I worked in a private hospital I would earn quite a lot more, but I'm very happy where I am, and I enjoy looking after children.

At the moment I still live with my parents, but I've just rented an apartment, and I shall be moving in there shortly. It has been very difficult for me to break away from my family. I get on very well with my parents, but I think at my age I'm old enough to look after myself. My parents are still not very happy about the

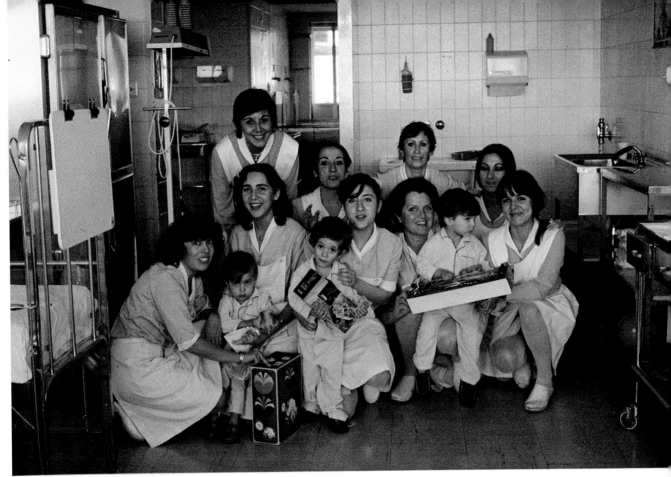

We try to create a homelike atmosphere in our ward.

idea, because to their way of thinking I should stay at home until I get married. But I'm not sure when or if I will ever get married. I'm financially independent so I can lead my own life.

It was possible to live very cheaply at home and I took advantage of this to save up. Every summer I used to go on marvelous vacations. I've been all over Asia, India, North Africa, and Mexico, besides Europe. Now that I've got to support myself completely, I don't think I'll be able to afford vacations like those any more.

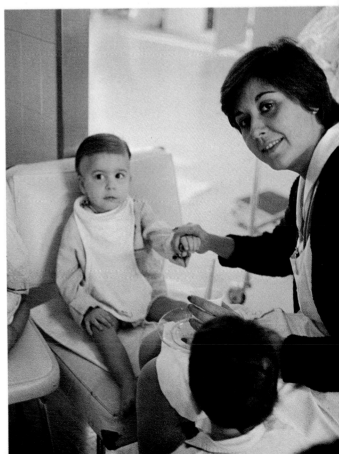

Sometimes I really have to coax the children to take their medicine.

"The French try to burn our trucks"

José Ramon Alonso is 38 and has been a long-distance truck driver for sixteen years. His home is in Gijón, in the province of Asturias, although he spends most of his time on the road.

I've been a long-distance truck driver for sixteen years, working for most of the time on international routes. I work for a transportation company based in Pamplona, the capital of Navarra. It has branches all over Spain and in most countries in Europe, so I don't necessarily have to go to Pamplona to pick up my load.

Recently, I've been on a run to England. I take a wide variety of cargoes over, ranging from products such as

My truck is like a second home, and I sleep very well in the bed I have behind the seats.

refrigerators, books, and shoes, to fruit — especially oranges. It takes me about eighteen hours to get to England. I normally go on the expressways through France to Calais. This makes the journey much faster, although you have to pay to use them and they are pretty expensive. I sometimes have trouble in the south of France. The farmers there are up in arms about Spanish fruit and vegetables being imported into the Common Market. Even if I'm not carrying fruit I'm sometimes held up for hours. Whenever the French start trying to burn and destroy our trucks, we all have to wait at the frontier for the French police to escort us through the troubled area in convoys.

I don't think this problem will be solved even when Spain joins the Common Market. The Spanish fruit and vegetable crops are always earlier than the French crops because of the warmer climate in Spain. This means we can supply the ever-increasing demands of Germany, Holland and England before the French. I don't think anyone can do anything about changing the climate!

My home is in Gijón in the province of Asturias. It's an important fishing port and a beautiful city. I own a butcher's shop there, which is run by my wife. One of the problems with being a long-distance driver, is that I'm away from home a lot of the time. If we lived in Pamplona, I would see my wife more often – about once a week. But as it is, a month or six weeks might go by between each visit to Gijón. Even then I might be at home for only one or two days. You really have to like this job, or else you wouldn't put up with it.

My company has about seventy drivers on its permanent staff and also contracts out work to about a hundred independent drivers, who own their own trucks. I prefer to work for a regular fixed wage and not have to worry about paying for my own trucks, which would be very expensive – between 7–8 million pesetas ($52,000–59,000). Even though you can get a loan to pay for it, the repayments are very difficult to meet.

The biggest problem I have when I'm driving in foreign countries is language. I can speak a little bit of English, German, and French, but not really enough to have a conversation. People abroad are normally very helpful when I ask them how to get somewhere. More than once they have gone out of their way to take me there.

I find English food very different from Spanish food and hard to get used to. I like French food a bit better, but I'm always glad to get back here and have a good meal.

Setting out from Pamplona on one of my trips to England.

"My university has 50,000 students"

Pilar Garcia Jordan, 31, was born in Esquedas, a small town in the province of Huesca. She now lives and works in Barcelona, where she is a lecturer in history at the university.

I'm a lecturer in modern and contemporary history at the Central University of Barcelona. I give lectures twice a week — on Tuesdays and Thursdays. The other days I spend doing research and preparing my lectures.

I started my career as a primary school teacher, but the work didn't really satisfy

In Galicia, the green fields go right down to the sea.

me and so I decided to go and take a university course in history. It is very difficult to get a grant to go to a university (only 3 percent of students receive grants). Since my parents couldn't afford to support me during the five years that the degree course lasted, I had to work as a teacher during the day and go to college in the evenings. This was very difficult. Correcting the children's books took up a lot of time outside school, so it was very hard to find time for my own studies.

Anyway, I finally got my degree, and was given a job at the university as an assistant lecturer. I wanted to become a lecturer, but first I had to write a thesis to obtain my doctorate. I wrote my thesis on the Church in Spain and how it affects everyday life.

The Church has always been very closely linked with the government in Spain, and it is only recently that the two "powers" have been separated. Catholicism is no longer the country's official religion (although it is still the most widespread), and people may now choose their own religion. In my opinion, the Church doesn't influence society as much as it did perhaps ten years ago. However, in certain regions of Spain, like Castilla (Castille), its presence is more obvious. But generally the ties between Catholics and the Church are not so strong, especially in the big cities. The new divorce law would never have been passed if the Catholic Church was still united with the government.

In Spain, most provinces have a university with an average of about 5,000 students, but the universities of Barcelona and Madrid are huge. My university has about 50,000 students and the two in Madrid have about 100,000 each. This is partly due to the size of the two cities and partly due to the fact that many young people prefer to go to a big university far away from their home. This allows them to be independent. For many Spanish parents are strict and like to keep their children at home where they can keep an eye on them until they get married.

I usually spend summer vacations traveling around Spain, but my favorite place is the Atlantic coast of Asturias and Galicia. The long, deserted sandy beaches and green fields which stretch right to the coast really capture my imagination. It's a region which hasn't been discovered by the tourists, so it's marvellous for a really restful holiday. It's also a good place for studying and writing. Part of my job as a lecturer is to do research and afterwards publish the results in book form. I find that while I'm working at the university, it's very difficult to get my thoughts organized to write a book.

This is the sort of place I stay in during my summer vacation – a typical Asturian farmhouse.

"I speak Catalan and Castilian"

Luis Hidalgo Orivé is 11 and lives with his parents and two sisters in an apartment in Barcelona. He goes to a school run by priests, where he enjoys playing hockey and learning languages. On weekends the family goes to its house in Papiol.

My parents have an apartment in central Barcelona, where we live for most of the year. I've got two sisters, one is thirteen and the other is seven years old. My school is quite close to our home so I walk there every day. We start at 8:40 a.m. and finish at 5:00 p.m.

It's a private school run by priests. Although it's quite expensive – 15,000 pesetas ($110) a month – I enjoy myself there and I take lots of sports.

People in different parts of Spain speak different languages, with local dialect variations. At school, most of the classes are given in Catalan, but some, such as Spanish literature and Spanish language, are given in Castilian. I can speak both Catalan and Castilian with no problem, although I am happier when I'm speaking in Catalan. It's strange, but you get accustomed to speaking to certain people in one language, and once you've got into the habit it's difficult to change. For example, in school I speak in Catalan. But with my parents and my sisters I speak in Castilian – although my parents speak to each other in Catalan. This may seem confusing, but it's very common. My parents perhaps wanted to teach us Castilian first, even though their common language was Catalan. Once they got used to talking to us in Castilian, however, they couldn't get out of the habit.

I like learning languages. I study French at school and I have private English lessons twice a week after school. On an average I have a couple of hours of homework to do every night, although sometimes I don't get around to finishing it. The thing I enjoy most about school is playing hockey on roller skates. We have two afternoons' training a week, and a game against another school every Saturday.

On Sundays our family often goes to Papiol, a small village 30 km (18 miles) from Barcelona, where my parents have a house. It's really great to be out in the country so I can ride a bike, climb trees and do all the things that I can't do at home in the city. In the summer I have about three months' vacation and we spend most of the time in Papiol. My father stays in Barce-

20

One of my favorite things at school is playing hockey on roller skates.

lona working, but he comes to visit us on weekends. He runs a bar and so he doesn't finish work until the early hours of the morning. At that time he doesn't feel like driving out to the country. There is a swimming pool in Papiol which we go to a lot in the summer. We don't go to the beach very much, although it's only about half-an-hour's trip by car. There are always so many people there that I prefer to stay in Papiol.

When I grow up I'd like to be a vet because I love animals, but I'm told I'll have to study for many years. I'm not sure I can manage that.

When we're in Papiol, I like playing with my sisters better than going to the beach.

"Machines have changed the mining industry"

José Hernandez Paterna, 35, was born in Cartagena, but now lives in Leon, where he works as a mining engineer. His job involves keeping a check on industrial safety measures.

After qualifying as a mining engineer, my first job was in a coal mine in Asturias, near Oviedo, which is the most important coal region in Spain. At one time, many mines were closed down because they had become unprofitable, but now they are being reopened because of the energy crisis. These days, the idea of a miner with a pick and a spade is very out of date. Modern machinery and earthmoving

The typical "miner with a pick and spade" hardly exists any more. Machines have taken over.

equipment has completely changed the mining industry. Now, fewer men are needed to do the work. For example, in the time it took ten men to mine a hundred tons of coal, one man and a machine can mine twice as much. This means that there are fewer miners, but that they are better paid. A miner can earn up to 130,000 pesetas ($956) a month, depending on the hours he works. Since most of them live in small villages, they haven't got much to spend their money on.

Safety in mines has improved a great deal, due to better ventilation and the fact that explosives are no longer used. When I worked in Asturias, I became interested in safety and the prevention of accidents. This led me to find a job with the Ministry of Public Works. My department deals with the investigation of accidents and inspection of safety measures used in industry. In this way I have a chance to visit all types of industry, but particularly mines. At the moment I'm based in Leon.

Some of the mines I visit are among the main sources of mercury in the world.

These mines are particularly dangerous due to the vapors produced by mercury. These can be absorbed into the body through the skin. The men work for only two or three hours a day, three days a week, and a strict watch is kept on their health.

When I'm not out on inspection tours, my working day starts at 7:45 a.m. and finishes at 3:15 p.m. – so I have a lot of the afternoon free. I make the most of the time by going to university, where I am getting a degree in Art History. I enjoy painting as a hobby.

Sometimes I organize trips to visit a mine for my fellow students and the lecturers. The other day I went with a group to a potassium and salt mine. They were all very surprised to travel through the tunnels

Sometimes I organize visits to mines for fellow students and teachers at my university.

in a jeep and find themselves in huge caverns dug out of the rock. They had expected something very different. The potassium is mainly used for ferti- lizers and explosives.

I'm also interested in solar energy and I've installed some solar panels on the roof of my house. The possibilities for using solar energy have not yet been fully in- vestigated. However, a lot of research is going on in Almeria, which has the greatest number of hours of sunshine per year in the whole of Spain. I think that with future scientific advances, Spain will soon be able to take more advantage of its famous sunshine.

"Leather is an important industry in Spain"

Loly Dominguez, 27, works in a leather and fur factory in Bilbao. She started work as a secretary because she was good at languages, but now has responsibility for managing many different aspects of the business.

I began working for this company as a secretary in the export department. I can speak French, English and German, so I was able to help out with foreign clients. Gradually I took on more responsibilities and now I look after marketing, design, sales, trade fairs and publicity. I try and do all this during normal working hours (8:30 a.m.–2:00 p.m. and 4:00 p.m.–7:30 p.m.).

I've organized a room in my apartment into a studio where I can do my painting.

But every day it gets more difficult to find time for everything. It's not very common in Spain for a woman to be part of management in a company, and in fact I'm not officially head of any department I just do the work.

My company is divided into two sections. One part produces leather from cow and pig hides, which is sold to the shoe manufacturers and the leather trade. The other part makes sheepskins and rabbit skins into overcoats and jackets. Most of this clothing is exported. This industry grew up in Spain because we have abundant supplies of rabbit- and sheep-skins. Also, labor is relatively cheap here.

Recently, massive amounts of uncured skins have been exported to Korea to be made up, since labor is even cheaper there. This has made the price of raw materials soar, and apart from that, there are very few skins left to buy. These things could put an end to the industry in Spain.

Our factory also makes fur coats from mink, fox and astrakhan (a Russian sheep), but these are imported furs.

The shoe trade, to which a large proportion of our cured leather is sold, is a very important industry in Spain. We export shoes to all parts of Europe, especially England, and also to the United States and South America.

My hobby is painting, which I find very relaxing. At weekends or in any free time I can find during the day, I like to slip away to my apartment, where I've organized a small room as a mini-studio.

My grandparents live on a small farm in the mountains not far from Bilbao. Whenever I can, I like to go and stay with them. There I can enjoy a world which has changed very little over the past fifty years.

I'm married with one child — a four-year-old girl. I find it very difficult to combine being a wife and mother with a full-time job. Even though my husband and I are both working, we always make time to have lunch and dinner together at home with our daughter. After work, my husband goes to the university, where he's taking a degree in economics. He's already got two degrees, but studying is his hobby. As a result he's always very busy, so he relies on me to do all the housework and look after our daughter. Despite the fact that more and more women are going out to work, in general it is still the wife who is expected to look after the home.

My grandparents are traditional farmers. I enjoy going to stay on their farm near Bilbao.

"My designs vary from region to region"

Octavio Torres, 35, is an architect working in Salamanca. He designs houses for people in all parts of Spain, adapting his houses to the different climate in each region.

In my work as an architect, I have had to travel all over Spain and so I've really got to know the basic differences between the various regions of Spain. These differences include language, climate, culture and traditions. In my opinion, the architecture of a region adapts to the way of life there.

I have always designed houses which take into account the way people will live in them, and not just to look good. A home must be practical. If I'm designing a house in Galicia, for example, where the weather is mainly cold and wet, I can't use the same ideas I might have used for a house in Andalucia, where it's hot for ninety per cent of the time.

I always try to use traditional designs, but incorporate modern features and techniques. The traditional design is one which has evolved over a period of centuries. By a system of trial and error, people have arrived at the most suitable style for each region.

I wouldn't say there is one particular style of Spanish architecture, because it is so varied from one region to another. In Andalucia the fierce sun means that my main problem is keeping the inside of a house cool. So, the houses I design are normally built round an interior patio which very often has a fountain in the middle, surrounded by shrubs and trees. All the rooms of the house look or open out on to the patio – which is shady and cool. The houses are usually whitewashed, as white reflects the heat and makes the house cooler. In Galicia and Cantabria, which are on the Atlantic coast, my problem is quite the reverse. Most of the time it is wet and cold. Houses have to be designed so that most things can be done inside. The rooms are larger and the windows are bigger in order to let in as much light as possible. The fireplace is a very important feature because people spend a lot of their time in front of it. The whole design is geared towards cosiness and warmth.

On the north Mediterranean coast, from Valencia up to the French border, the heat is not so intense. Here I design a house

Basque country houses tend to be big enough to accommodate animals at ground floor level, under the living quarters.

bearing in mind that the owners will spend a lot of time outside. There is often a patio at the back of the house, where the children can play and you can sit out and laze in the sun.

In the Pyrenees, it's a bit like being in Switzerland, so the houses are built to stand up to extremely cold weather and snow. You have to make sure of good insulation against the cold, and build steep-sloping roofs, so that the snow doesn't collect on them too much.

So, all in all, it's very important for me to know exactly where I've got to build the house, before I start designing it.

Narrow streets of whitewashed houses, with lots of potted plants on the balconies, are very typical of Cordoba.

"It's difficult to make ends meet"

Josep Solé is 66 and runs a farm in Caldas de Malavella, in the province of Gerona. He has had to reorganize his farm completely over the last ten years, as all his tenant farmers have given up farming.

I'm a farmer, or "worker of the land," as I prefer to call myself. My farm is in Cataluña in the northeast of Spain. Farms are very much affected by their location. Spain is a big country and the geographical, climatic and cultural conditions vary enormously from one region to another. In provinces such as Galicia, which is very poor, you have *minifundios*,

The tenant farmer's son is collecting the stalks of maize after harvesting.

tiny landholdings which are really too small to make a profit. In provinces such as Andalucia and Castilla, there are huge estates called *latifundios*, where half the land is owned by a tiny minority of the farmers. These *latifundios* mean that the vast majority of farmers are, in fact, farm-laborers. They don't own the land and only work in the olive-picking and harvesting season. So, although there are a few very rich landowners, the region is poor and underdeveloped. Both the *minifundios* and the *latifundios* have brought unemployment, and many people have moved to the richer provinces of Spain and to Europe.

I'm perhaps a typical Catalan farmer, with a medium-sized farm of 100 hectares (250 acres). Up until a few years ago, my farm was worked in the traditional Catalan way. It was divided into *masoverias* (tenant farms), each of about 15 hectares (37 acres). The rent for these farms is normally paid in kind – that is to say the crop is divided so one third goes to the owner and the tenant keeps the rest. The decision on what crop to sow is usually taken jointly, because both want a profitable harvest.

My main crop is wheat, which is the main crop in Spain as a whole. Small crops of barley, oats and maize are grown, and we have to import these cereals to cover our needs. The central region of Spain – la Mancha – is the biggest producer of cereals. Like most farmers, I sell my cereals through the state organization, which offers a guaranteed price. It is not obligatory, but it is easier to use this system.

The guaranteed price is, in my opinion, very low, and as we hardly receive any subsidies, it is very difficult to make ends meet. This has hit the small masover (tenant farmer) the hardest. Of the five masovers I had a few years ago, I have only one left and he will be leaving shortly. The land is not profitable any more and everybody is leaving to work in industry.

Obviously I have had to reorganize my farm in view of these changes. I decided to specialize in cereals rather than in cattle, which require more manpower. I sow these crops on half my land, and turn the remaining half over to forestry. I plant fast-growing trees such as the plane, which takes about twenty years to grow, rather than the pine, which takes between eighty and a hundred years to grow. Pine is used for making furniture and you can get a good price for it, but it doesn't compensate for having to wait eighty years to receive your money! I sell timber direct to the sawmills, and from there it goes to make paper, laminates for furniture, or wooden boxes for use in industry. I've also invested in modern machinery, which means that the farm can basically be worked by one man – except when I rent a combine harvester for three days at harvest time.

As is the tradition, my eldest son will inherit the farm and work it by himself. In fact, since I broke my leg in a car accident, most of the work is done by him already. My other two children have received a university education to give them a good start in other careers.

Here I am with the tenant's wife and her grandson. We are checking to see if the maize (corn) is ready to be harvested.

"The Spanish like a gamble"

Rogelio Gimenez, 42, is a lottery salesman in Zaragoza. He has been blind since birth. Thanks to this job he can be financially independent and enjoy everyday contact with other people.

I've been blind since birth and I work as a lottery salesman. If you come to Spain, it's more than likely that you will see, standing near the entrance to a market, or on a street corner, a blind person with sheets of tickets pinned to his jacket. He is selling the *cupon*, a ticket for a daily lottery which is organized by the *Organizacion Nacional de Ciegos Espanoles* (the Spanish Organization for the Blind).

In Spain, the blind are not looked after by the social services, but by an organization run by the blind for the blind. This organization plays a very big part in my life – as it does for most blind people here. Thanks to the lottery, I have a job and a chance to be financially independent. Through the organization, I am able to participate in many activities especially arranged for the blind. They include sports, music (many of us play in orchestras) and general social activities.

My working day depends very much on how quickly I sell my quota of *cupons*, but normally I spend about eight hours in the street. This is pretty tough when the weather is cold, but there is always the compensation that you are in touch with other people. I tend to get a regular clientele who always come to buy their *cupon* from me. We usually have a little chat, which is very important to me, because it makes my day more interesting. Being blind can make you feel isolated, so I enjoy the contact I have with the public.

First thing in the morning, I go down to the offices where I buy the *cupons*. If I don't sell them all, I can always take them back and get a refund, as long as I do so before 8 p.m. when the lottery takes place. My average earnings each day amount to 3,500 pesetas ($26). This depends on the number of *cupons* I sell, because I get a commission on each one. The price of a *cupon* is 25 pesetas (19 cents) and out of this I receive about 8 pesetas. Part is held back as a provision for vacations and health insurance. To earn 3,500 pesetas a day, I have to sell about 450 *cupons*. As they are cheap, many people buy several,

which makes my work easier. I'm thankful that the Spanish have always liked to do a little gambling. You can win 6,500 pesetas ($48) on a 25-peseta ticket – not a fortune, but then it's a very cheap gamble anyway. The blind lottery must not be confused with the state lottery, which is much more expensive and gives out prize money amounting to millions.

Every day I take up my place at the entrance to the market.

Through our lottery we are able to finance special schools for the blind of all ages, from kindergarten to university. We have special training centers for physiotherapists, switchboard operators and so forth where visual skills are not the most important part of the job. We also have our own health service.

But it is difficult to find work, and that is why over 11,000 blind people sell the lottery tickets. I've taken special courses in order to find a "better" job, but the truth is I earn a good living as a salesman and I haven't been able to find a job which can equal the money.

Many lottery salesmen set up their little tables in the street.

"It's not fair to call our wine 'jug wine'"

Juan Muria, 37, runs his own wine shop, and is also director of a small vineyard. He is very proud of Spanish wine, and is trying hard to abolish its bad reputation. He lives in Logrono, in northern Spain.

My work in the wine trade deals with everything from the vineyards to the customer in the shop. I'm technical director of a small vineyard and I also run a specialized wine shop. In Spain, you can buy wine from grocers, who sell a limited range of well-known brands, or from *bodegas*, which are a cross between a bar and a wine shop. *Bodegas* are normally stacked full of big casks of wine and you can either have a glass of wine straight

Before ordering wine for my shop, I travel around the country inspecting the grapes.

from the barrel, or fill up a bottle to take home with you. So a specialist shop like mine is not very common, even though wine is considered to be our national drink.

The Spanish climate is very good for growing grapes – we have more vineyards than any other country in the world. There are innumerable small vineyards which produce their own wine. Many of the wines are very good, but virtually unknown to the general public. In my shop I offer a wide range of wines – not just the famous ones – and in order to do this I have to travel around the country.

The old traditional methods of making wine have almost disappeared, but the process is not totally mechanized. A good wine can never be made by a machine. One stage of winemaking involves blending the juice from various batches of crushed grapes. In my job as technical director of the vineyard, I have to assess the different *caldos* (brews) and decide which ones to mix. I must also judge what amount of each chosen *caldo* is needed to give the required taste.

I also help to organize "wine fairs", as I feel they are very important for the promotion of Spanish wine. Wine fairs aim to encourage people to buy more wine, and to try out different varieties. Fairs are usually held in the provincial capitals. Most of the local vineyard owners will set up stalls in a particular street. People can buy an entry ticket for about 100 pesetas (75 cents). This gives them the right to taste ten wines.

It's really not fair to judge all Spanish wine by the poor image that it has in many foreign countries. We produce some very good-quality wine in Spain. The problem is that we've got this reputation because for years the only wine that was exported was the poor-quality, cheap, unmatured wine. This was transported by tanker (like oil!) to countries such as England, where it was bottled and sold as "Spanish wine." I'm happy to say that the last time I was in England, I saw that in some of the wine shops it is now possible to buy what I'd call a bottle of "real" Spanish wine, and not just cheap jug wine.

Wine is made from either black or green grapes – black for red wine and green for white wine. Certain particular varieties of grape make the best wine. One of the most famous Spanish red wines, *Rioja*, is made from black grapes grown in Navarra, Logroño and Alava.

It's my job as technical director to taste the caldos *and decide how they should be blended.*

"Our democracy is still very young"

Joan Ganyet i Solé, 35, is a member of the autonomous Catalan Parliament. He comes from the mountain region of the Pyrenees near the French border. He decided to go into politics when democracy returned to Spain after Franco died.

By profession, I am an architect. But when democracy was reintroduced into Spain after the death of General Franco, I decided to make my own small contribution to the new system. I joined the *Partido Socialista de Cataluña* and I am now an elected member of the Catalan Parliament.

I think that to be able to understand the present situation in Spain, one has to look at Spain's recent history. In 1931 a democratic republic was formed, and King Alfonso XIII went into voluntary exile as a result. This was the second attempt to

The Catalan Parliament. Under the Franco regime it was a museum of modern art.

create a democratic republic in Spain. The first attempt lasted one year and was ended by a military coup in 1874.

During the five years that the republic lasted, Cataluña, Euskadi and Galicia were granted autonomy. Some of the new governments tried to bring about wide reforms, but the Fascist uprising in 1936 put a stop to this. Three years of civil war ended in a victory for the Fascists. As a result, Spain was governed by a dictatorship under General Franco, until his death.

This dictatorship brought severe repression, especially of regional cultures and languages, which is still hard for people to forget today. It also meant, of course, that Spain was cut off from the rest of Europe.

Things began to change with the arrival of millions of tourists during the 1960s. It was like the opening of a window towards Europe. After Franco's death in 1975, Juan Carlos de Borbon, grandson of Alfonso XIII, became king. He immediately called for democratic elections, and this was when I first became involved in politics, helping in the Socialist Party's electoral campaign.

The main task of the new government was to create a new constitution. In it, all the political parties recognized the existence of three "nations" in Spain — Euskadi, Cataluña and Galicia — and recognized their right to autonomous government. These three regions now have their own parliaments. In time autonomy will be given to other regions. In this way, Spain will become a federated state, with every nation or region having its own parliament under the central government in Madrid.

My own work as a member of the Catalan Parliament has mostly to do with the mountain regions of the Pyrenees, which is where I come from. Here life is hard, and

Life is very hard in the small widely-scattered villages of the Pyrenees – especially in winter.

the fact that there are many small, widely-scattered villages, makes the task of providing schools and medical services a real problem. Some people have to travel for four hours to reach a hospital.

Our democracy is still very young. Although important new laws have been passed, it will take a long time for the old regime to be completely forgotten. The change to democracy has taken place without disruptions. But this means that there are still many people from the old regime in the civil service and government circles. In my opinion this slows up the process of change.

35

"Olive oil prices are completely unrealistic"

Felipe Vilaseca, 65, is an olive grower in Castellón. If he hadn't inherited the land from his father, he wouldn't cultivate olives, as it is the least profitable form of agriculture.

Olive oil is one of Spain's most important products. Olive tree plantations can be found all along the Mediterranean coast, from Lerida and Tarragona in Cataluña, down to Jaen and Sevilla in Andalucia.

My family has owned a plantation of about 600 trees for many generations. I began working there with my father when I was eight. Now it's mine. I run it by

When the olives are nearly ripe, they turn a reddish-brown colour.

myself, as my sons have all left the village to get better jobs elsewhere. Obviously, at harvest time I can't do all the work myself, so I hire part-time workers during the two-month picking season.

The olive tree grows to a very great age – normally it is over a hundred years old. It's almost eternal, because if the upper part is rotten, you can cut it down and it will sprout again from the trunk. Olives are used mainly for making olive oil, although some are sold for eating. They may be used in salads or as *tapas* (cocktail snacks), in which case the pit is often taken out and the olive stuffed with tuna or anchovy. You may have eaten both green and black olives. The only difference between them is that the green one is picked in September when the olive is unripe. The black one is picked a couple of months later, when the olive is fully ripe. Black olives are used to make oil. The season for picking them starts in November and lasts for two to four months, depending on the region and the amount of olives to be picked.

When olives are picked, two large sheets

I get about 5 kilos (11 lb) of olives from each tree.

of plastic are placed under the tree on each side of the trunk, so that all the olives will fall onto the plastic. Then the olives may be pulled off the branches with a sort of wooden hand on the end of a long pole – which is what I do. Or the branches are knocked with a pole until the olives fall to the ground. The exact system of picking varies from one region to another.

I take the olives to the factory where they are cleaned and crushed into a paste. From this paste about 35–40 per cent of the oil is separated. This is the best-quality olive oil. The paste then goes through hydraulic presses which extract the remaining oil. This is still good oil, but it's a bit more acidic and has a slightly different taste from the oil of the first pressing.

Around here, you would be considered a big landowner if you owned 3,000 olive trees, but in Andalucia some of them own 80,000 trees. In Andalucia the majority of the farm laborers can only find work in the olive-picking season from November to March. For the rest of the year they are out of work or they have to go to France or Switzerland to find a job picking grapes. Some pick fruit in other regions of Spain.

If I hadn't inherited my olive plantation from my father, I would never have chosen to grow olives, because it is the least profitable form of agriculture. The price farmers get for olive oil is fixed by the government and it is completely unrealistic. From one of my olive trees I get about 5 kilos (11 lb) of oil. The price I get for it varies from 100–150 pesetas (75 cents to $1.10) for about 2 pounds, depending on the quality. So I get about 750 pesetas ($5.50) from a tree, but that doesn't take into consideration the cost of fertilizers.

"Criminals don't work an eight-hour day"

Sebastian Ruiquelme, 29, joined the Guardia Civil after finishing his military service. After serving as a frontier guard and in traffic control, he asked to be transferred to Asturias, where he was born.

One of the advantages of my profession is that I can follow it anywhere I may choose to live in Spain. I was drawn by Asturias, with its gentle valleys and green hills. I was born here. My parents had a house on the hillside in a range of mountains called "Los Picos de Europa."

As a child, I would often come across the local pair of Guardias Civiles out on patrol while I was chasing rabbits in the wood with my dog. The sight of them coming down the track always filled me with a certain awe, which later changed to friendship when I got to know them better. It was through them that I learnt about the Guardia Civil – its tradition and duties. In the end I decided to join up once I'd done my military service.

The Guardia Civil was founded many years ago, in 1844. At that time the country-side was plagued by bandits and thieves. The Guardia Civil is a type of police force composed of about 70,000 men and has a basically military structure. In general, it looks after rural areas, although ports, airports, frontiers and the coastline also come under its control. In capital cities, police duties are carried out by the national police and the *Cuerpo Superior de Policia*, which is a detective force similar to the FBI in the United States.

When I graduated from the training academy, I was sent to a frontier post. My job was to stop smuggling and to keep a check on everyone entering and leaving the country. I was then transferred to La Coruña in Galicia, where I joined the traffic section. Although the barracks were in the city, we carried out our patrols and duties on the national highways outside the city, keeping an eye on all the cars and trucks and making sure they obeyed the highway code. We receive first-aid training and we often had to make use of it, because when an accident occurred we were frequently the first on the scene.

There are many specialist branches of the Guardia Civil. They include the mountain rescue unit, formed by expert skiers and climbers, and the underwater unit of frogmen and divers, who carry out rescue missions at sea or in rivers.

When I got married, my wife and I decided that we wanted to live in a small village. Since I had always wanted to return to Asturias, I asked to be transferred here. In my village there are four Guardias Civiles and we all live together with our families in the *Casa-Cuartel*, which is typical here. It is a building which includes the offices and cells of a normal police station and the living quarters for the families of the Guardias in the garrison.

My duties consist mainly of patrolling the district, either on foot or in a landrover – depending on the route for the day. This *Correria*, as it is called, keeps us in touch with the isolated farms. We are also able to keep a check on the many weekend cottages in the district, which are empty most of the time. Officially I'm on duty eight hours a day, but very often circumstances mean that the hours are much longer. Criminals don't work an eight-hour day, so we have to be prepared to carry out our responsibility for protecting life and property at all hours.

There are always two of us when we go on patrol. That is why we are called la pareja – *the couple.*

La pareja *on traffic control duty.*

39

"There are very few of us left"

Felix Martin, 40, is a stonemason in the small village of Floresta, near Lerida. He is afraid that the old crafts are being lost and so has written a book about his profession.

Craftsmen like myself, who work in the traditional way, are becoming very scarce in Spain. My village was once famous for its sandstone quarries and for the hand-cut stone that was produced by our stonemasons.

A few years ago our village had a population of 650. Now we are only 160. Most of the younger generation leave to find work in the cities, because there is none for them here. Now, machines have taken over the

I have my own quarry and so I can make sure I get exactly the stone I want.

stone-cutting jobs which were once done by people. Of the forty-five quarries that used to be worked around here, mine is the only one left. Apart from my father, I am the only stonemason still working by hand. Other stonemasons have set up factories, cutting stone with machines. To me, they have become mechanics rather than craftsmen.

Stone which has been cut by a machine never has the same appearance as stone worked by hand. A machine can never have the "feel" that a craftsman has for the stone he is working, or appreciate its faults or its beauty. Very often, machine-cut stone is so perfectly cut that it could have come out of a mould – as if it were made of plastic.

Everthing I know about stone I learned from my father. He has never claimed to be a great artist or sculptor. But sometimes I wonder if there really is any difference between a good stonemason and a sculptor. Perhaps it's that a stonemason tends to make functional objects such as fireplaces and lintels for doors and windows, rather than purely decorative objects.

In Spain many of our palaces and churches are beautifully decorated with cut stone. A lot of my work comes from such places, because there is always restoration work to be done. This has to be a perfect copy of the original stone. Obviously they can't go to a factory, which only produces standard pieces of stone. These jobs are always given to stonemasons like myself. For this reason I don't think stonemasons will disappear completely, although there are very few of us left. I've done several jobs for the monastery in Poblet, which dates back to the twelfth century; also for the monastery of Santes Creus, which was founded at about the same time.

I don't think I'm ever going to get rich by working as a stonemason, because I think that a good craftsman is never a good businessman. I enjoy my work and for me that is more important than anything else, but these days that sort of philosophy is uncommercial. However, I'm very happy as I am. My wife and children understand and accept this, and with my wife working as a hairdresser we manage to get by.

Recently, I took a holiday for the first time in my life. I didn't go away anywhere — I just spent two weeks working on a sculpture I'd designed myself. This was like a holiday for me. I've always been very patriotic about Cataluña, although I don't belong to a political party, and I wanted this sculpture to reflect my feelings. It is of a cross which touches the ground with one of its arms. There are three motifs on the cross. One is of Montserrat, which symbolizes the spirit of Cataluña. Another is a sign of victory, which symbolizes the triumph of Cataluña. And the third is Saint George, the patron saint of Cataluña. I don't known when I'll find time to do any more of my own sculptures, but if I do I might organize an exhibition one day.

I have written a book, which was published recently, about my village and the profession of stonemasonry. I feel that my village represents a world that is disappearing. I wanted to put everything I know down on paper so that it wouldn't be lost forever. I've always believed in supporting the arts, so I help students who are doing research on the region or on community life in villages.

I made this sculpture for pleasure, to reflect my feelings about Cataluña.

"The Basque people want more autonomy"

Begonia Foruria Atxaval, 34, was born in Bilbao, where she is now bringing up a family and teaching sailing at weekends. She feels there is no easy solution to the problems of the Basque country.

Nobody living in Euskadi (the Basque country) is unaware of the difficult times we are going through. The question of our independence from Spain splits families because feelings run very high. Talks between the two sides are very difficult, as nobody wants to betray their ideals.

My family has always believed strongly in Basque traditions and culture. I was brought up speaking Euskara (Basque),

Before we had children, my husband and I used our boat to compete in regattas (races).

which is totally different from any of the European languages. It is said to date back to before 2000 B.C., making it the oldest of the European languages. I only began speaking Castilian when I went to my first communion at the age of eight.

I took a teacher-training course when I left school and began teaching the Basque language in *ikostolas*, which are special Basque-speaking schools. Up until 1965, these schools were prohibited and the classes were held in private houses with desks for about fifteen children. It was all very rudimentary and you couldn't really call them schools in the normal sense. These days the schools are permitted, but there is now only one school for the whole of Bilbao.

The Basque nationalist movement began at the beginning of this century and called for more self-government. This movement was more of a patriotic organization than a political one. It was only recently, in the 1960s, when the E.T.A. (*Euskadi ta Askatasuna* – Basque Country and Freedom Party) was formed, that the movement split

into different parties and separate aims. E.T.A. is a clandestine organization of Marxist tendency. It fights for total independence for the Basque country – often using violent means to achieve its ends.

There are two legal nationalist parties. *Herri Batasuna* is a radical left-wing nationalist party, which fights for far-reaching independence through legal channels. The *Partido Nacionalista Vasco* (Basque Nationalist Party) is politically conservative. The P.N.V. also wants independence, but it believes in working for a solution through talks with the central government in Madrid.

Few people want to be governed by the parliament in Madrid (as was shown in the general elections), and many people aren't happy with the autonomy which has been given to Euskadi, because they feel it doesn't go far enough.

All the political parties in the Basque parliament continue to pressure Madrid to increase the scope of our self-government. As a result, popular support for E.T.A. has decreased, because people now feel that

I teach children to sail in boats called "Optimists", which are easy to handle.

their claims can be fulfilled by diplomatic means.

On an industrial level, things are very different. In the last 150 years Euskadi has changed from being one of the poorest parts of Spain, to being one of the richest. The steel industry is centered here, together with many other types of industry. This means that there are close trade links between Euskadi and the rest of Spain, so I doubt that the industrialists are very eager for Euskadi to become too independent.

I don't take an active part in politics. Since I've got three young children to look after, I've given up my work as a teacher until they're a bit older. Looking after the children is, in my opinion, more tiring than a full-time job. I'm also a sailing instructor and I give classes to children and teenagers on weekends.

My husband is also a keen sailor and we have a nine meter yacht. We used to compete in races before we had children, but now we just go on quiet cruises.

"Tourists only want a suntan"

Manolo Murciano is 27 and comes from Almeria. Now living in Madrid, he is working as a tourist guide, and finds that most visitors to Spain are not interested in getting to know the country.

I come from a small village in Almeria. I lived there until I was seventeen and I'd finished my basic education. I had always wanted to travel, so I decided to study tourism. Going to college was also a good opportunity for me to leave home – as I found life in my village very boring. Most of the young people there went off to the cities, either to go to college, or in the hope of getting a better job. There aren't many jobs in a country village, apart from farming, and that didn't appeal to me.

There wasn't a college nearby where I could study tourism, so I went to Madrid. I studied there for two years, paying my way through college by working in a bar in my spare time. My diploma in tourism means that I could set up a travel agency if I wanted to, but for the moment I prefer to work as a guide. I get well paid for showing tourists around Madrid. I take them to the Prado Museum, which contains one of the greatest collections of paintings in the world, or to the *Rastro*, the traditional open-air market. But what I enjoy most is taking visitors to out-of-the-way places

that a tourist would not normally find, such as small bars where the locals drop in for *tapas* (snacks) and a glass of wine.

In winter, when I haven't got much work as a guide, I work in a restaurant run by a friend of mine in Madrid. I do some of the cooking and serve in the bar.

One year I spent the summer working in the tourist information office in Torremolinos. Torremolinos has really grown as a tourist resort in the last twenty years. Hundreds of tower-block hotels have sprung up to cater to the thousands of tourists who come here for our famous Spanish sunshine. I found that, generally, the tourists weren't very interested in getting to know Spain; getting a suntan was much more important!

Exploring Spain is perhaps difficult if you're only here for a couple of weeks. But there are many places, especially in the center of the country, which are worth making the effort to see. Places such as Segovia and Caceres will give you a glimpse of our past and a view of Spanish life you won't get in a tourist resort.

For the tourists, the beaches and the hot Spanish sun are the two greatest attractions.

In the winter I work in a restaurant, where I do some of the cooking.

For me, some of the most interesting places to see are to be found in Andalucia. The Alhambra Palace in Granada, the mosque in Cordoba, and Las Reales Alcazares in Sevilla are all beautiful examples of Islamic art. They reflect the influence Arab culture has had on Spain. The Arabs conquered and ruled a large part of Spain for 900 years, and this has left its mark on our people as well as our architecture.

Tourism has given a good boost to our economy and has changed poor fishing villages into prosperous resorts. Now we are trying to improve our "cheap package holiday in a Spanish resort" image by offering better quality and service. And we are promoting tourism in regions of Spain that are off the beaten track.

"I'm carrying on a tradition"

Marcel Bergues, 41, was born in Valencia and first worked as a graphic artist, but for the past six years he has been producing hand-painted ceramic tiles. Many of the techniques he uses date back more than 800 years.

I've been a graphic designer since I was seventeen. My first job was for an advertising agency in Barcelona. Later I worked for various publishers illustrating books,

Painting the name of a shop on tiles can be more difficult than you think.

especially children's stories. Just over six years ago I became interested in ceramics and I decided to move to Manises, which is famous the world over for its ceramics. Manises is about 20 km (12 miles) from Valencia – where I was born. They have been making ceramics here for over 800 years and many of the traditional techniques are still used.

The mural which I am working on at the moment is made in exactly the same way as those which adorn the ancient mosques of the Arab world. It is 5 meters (16ft) long and was commissioned by one of the local yacht clubs to decorate their entrance hall. The subject is a view of a port.

Ceramic tiles are made from mineral soils which vitrify (turn glassy) when they are placed in a kiln (oven). I decorate them with a paint made from a powder of mineral oxides. These often change color completely in the kiln. One of the biggest problems with this sort of decoration is that I can't correct anything that I do, as the "paint" can't be rubbed out or covered up in any way. Another problem is that tiles

I'm just finishing a five-meter (16-ft) mural made of tiles, for a local yacht club.

may warp or crack in the kiln. Then I must re-do each tile, repeating the same design and color exactly, so that it will fit in perfectly with the rest. So you can imagine that the simple job of painting the name of a shop on ceramic tiles is not really very easy.

In Manises, many craftsmen work by themselves. Others like me form small teams of three or four people, but there are also more than 300 factories which produce ceramic and glazed tiles. Apart from being one of the world's major production centers, the town has an internationally famous school specializing in the study of ceramic art and its techniques.

As we have abundant supplies of tiles, they are used a great deal in the building trade. I don't mean the hand-painted tiles, but the ordinary glazed kind which are used for floors or on walls in kitchens and bathrooms. Apart from being very easy to clean, floor tiles keep the house cool, whereas carpets tend to give warmth. For this reason it is very common for people to tile their floors rather than have fitted carpets. In winter, they cover them with rugs, which can be taken up in the summer.

I also paint individual tiles, often with traditional designs or with people in regional dress. These may be added to a wall of plain glazed tiles to make it more decorative.

I enjoy my work immensely – and the fact that I'm carrying on a tradition begun by craftsmen so many years ago gives me great satisfaction.

"Teaching is a vocation"

Milagros Vera Lopez, 40, decided at an early age that she wanted to teach. She is now headmistress (principal) of a state school in Cuenca, but must rely on the parents to help overcome the shortage of facilities.

My father had a distillery for making aromatic products for use in perfumes, and our family was really quite well off. My parents wanted me to be a doctor or an architect, but I always wanted to teach. Despite the fact that I went to a private

None of the classes in my school has more than thirty-five pupils.

school run by nuns, I had a lot of contact with the state school in Cuenca, because my godmother was the headmistress there and it was she who stimulated my interest in teaching.

So I took a teacher-training course, specializing in music and English. I finished this when I was seventeen and began working in the ministry of education in Madrid, teaching English. I was then transferred to a small village school in the province of Cuenca, which was one of the most worthwhile experiences of my teaching career. Life was very basic and every morning the children came to school with two logs of wood for the fire. Our school had very few resources, but it was here that I began to appreciate the real importance of the work of a teacher.

After that I taught in various schools in different towns, until finally I became headmistress of a state school in the city of Cuenca. I got married here, and at the moment two of my children come to my school.

State education is totally free to the

pupils, but we don't receive enough money from the government to do everything that we would like. So I have reached an agreement with the parents' association, by which they pay a little money into a fund every month. With this money I am able to do many things. I can pay for an art teacher to come three times a week; build up a library for the school; set up a laboratory for practical science classes; and organize activities such as concerts, school outings and competitions.

However, at the moment a large proportion of Spanish children go to private schools because there aren't enough places in the state schools. Some private schools are subsidized by the government, but parents still have to pay quite substantial fees. Curiously, my school is not completely full – none of the classes has more than 35 pupils. So we're able to accept any pupil who applies. Normally, one has to make restrictions, with priority given to the children who live in the district and to the brothers and sisters of children at the school.

At the moment, there is very little un-employment among schoolteachers. But it will soon come, as there has been an avalanche of people who are entering the profession due to high unemployment in other sectors. This will probably change things quite a lot. Up to now, school-teachers have been predominantly women – five schoolmistresses to one school-master. This gives the men a great advantage, since boys are normally taught by men and the girls by women. The men can pick and choose which school they want to work in.

Teaching is a vocation – at least it is for me. I think this must be true in general, because, although salaries have been in-creased recently, we are still paid less than a skilled manual worker. I think teachers should be paid more, because teachers should be able to do a bit of traveling to improve their general knowledge. We also need to buy books and magazines to keep ourselves well informed. At the moment we can't afford to do these things.

A religious studies lesson. Today the children learn about all religions, not just Roman Catholicism.

"I've never been to school in my life"

Sebastian Santiago Aguilero, 41, has been training horses all his life. He comes from a gypsy family and runs some stables with his three brothers in Mazaro, Murcia.

I'm a gypsy – and proud of the fact. There are about 400,000 of us in Spain and we consider ourselves to be a different race from the rest of the population. We have our own customs and traditions – which some people call superstitions.

I've worked with horses and mules since I was ten years old. My family has always been in the horse trade, so I began my working life training mules for work in the fields. This went on until I was seventeen – in 1958 – when tractors were introduced and mules were no longer needed. (At that time the south was very backward compared with the rest of Spain.) I then changed to training horses.

I've never been to a school in my life and I'm not really a professional horse rider or trainer, because I've never received any sort of lessons. However, I've lived with horses all my life so I understand them – and after a while they understand me.

In Spain we have our own breed of horses called *El Caballo Español*, which originated in Andalucia. It's a very noble animal, extremely elegant and well-behaved. In my opinion, it's the most trustworthy breed of all. Once trained, these horses can be handled by a child. They don't frighten easily and are not temperamental like some English and Irish thoroughbreds.

I never try to train a horse before it's three years old. A younger horse is not really strong enough to take the weight of a rider. The weight can damage its legs and forelocks and in a short time make it

Here is a fine example of El Caballo Español, *with its broad neck and beautiful mane.*

When I first mount an unbroken horse, I'm always a bit wary.

elegant *paso español* (Spanish step). The horse picks up its legs very high as it walks or trots, keeping its head tucked back. I also teach horses to kneel and to sit down.

A Spanish horse is not very good at racing or jumping. The English and Irish horses are better at that. Recently though, English and Spanish horses have been interbred, producing very good results.

I run my stables with my three brothers. Gypsy families tend to stay together, with the eldest male taking charge. Since my father died my eldest brother has been head of the family, and very few decisions are taken without his consent. I'm the one who does most of the training, while my other brothers look after the buying and selling of the horses. The horses we have in the stables don't stay with us long. We buy untrained horses, train them, and then sell them at a reasonable profit. At the moment we own about fifty horses and look after another ten for their owners, who ride them on the weekends. I charge about 12,000 pesetas ($88) a month for their upkeep. We keep ten horses for hiring out, but we don't get much business except for foreign tourists in the summer. Up until a few years ago, only the very rich used to ride, except in Andalucia where horses have always been part of the way of life. But these days horseriding is becoming a popular hobby.

I always use the Spanish saddle when I train horses. I find it much more comfortable and I really wouldn't know how to handle an untrained horse with the flat English saddle.

If you wanted to buy a Spanish horse it would probably cost you between 150,000 and 200,000 pesetas ($1,100–$1,480). If you wanted the very best, however, you could pay from 2 to 5 million pesetas ($14,800–$37,000).

useless for riding. Normally, I take about three months to train a horse, although the time varies with each one. I begin by leading it with two long ropes, gaining its confidence by stroking and talking to it all the time. When I feel the horse is ready, I put a simple harness on it and later a saddle. I then start to ride it – for a little while each day – so bit by bit it gets used to having someone in the saddle.

This is the basic training. Later the horses undergo the *alta escuela* (high school) training, which includes the very

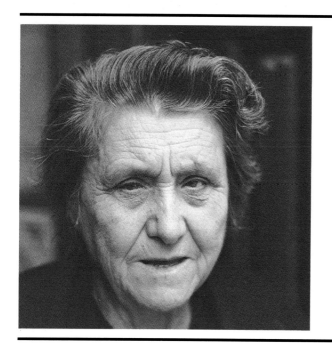

"Nine of us lived in three rooms"

Anita Cabello Barrea is now 80 and has been a caretaker in Madrid for the last twenty-five years. She brought up a family of ten children in Andalucia, but they eventually had to leave in order to find work.

Porteras (caretakers) are very much a part of city life, because most people live in apartments, and every apartment house has a *portera*. I've been working as a *portera* in Madrid for the last twenty-five years. In all that time my job hasn't changed very much, although now we are better paid. When I started in 1956 I was paid 850 pesetas ($6.25) a month. Now I'm earning 20,000 pesetas ($147). I only have to be on duty for eight hours a day, whereas in the early days I had to be on call from eight in the morning till ten at night.

I was born in Vinuela, a small town near Malaga, but my parents died when I was very young and I was sent to live with my grandparents in Granada. I got married when I was twenty-three and I had ten children. For many years, we worked a small plot of land leased to us by the agricultural institute, in exchange for sixty percent of all our crop. This land had been taken from the big landowners *(latifundistas)* in an attempt to share the land more fairly. But the land we were given was very poor and it was difficult to earn a living,

especially when so much of the crop was taken by the institute. In the end, the institute threw us off the land because they said we weren't working it properly.

So we decided to leave Andalucia, as there was very little possibility of finding work. I came to Madrid with nine of my children – one of my daughters had got married in Granada. My six sons got work immediately as laborers in the building trade, and this kept us going. A few years later I got this job. The living quarters are very small. There are two bedrooms (one with a kitchen in the corner) and a small living room where three people can barely sit down. Luckily, two of my sons got married here in Madrid, and so then I only had seven children living with me.

My little apartment may not sound like much, but then it was like heaven to me – a place I could call home, where at the same time I could earn a bit of money as a *portera*. I've always been very good at sewing, so I used to do embroidery work for people in the neighborhood to earn some extra money. Now my eyes aren't as good as they

used to be so I've had to give it up.

These days I have much more space as I only have one son living with me now – all the others are married. Sometimes I wonder how we ever fitted nine of us in before, and how I managed to do all the cooking in my tiny kitchen.

Apart from cleaning the staircase, opening the main door at 8 a.m. and locking it at 10 p.m., I don't have much work to do except to keep an eye on who comes into the building and ask them where they're going. Many *porteras* are terrific gossips. They like to know everything that happens in their building so that they can discuss the tenants with the other *porteras* on the street. I'm very much against this, because I respect the privacy of all my tenants and I like to consider them as friends.

As *porteras* used to be paid so little, all apartment houses had a *portera*, not just the luxury ones. Now that the law has fixed a minimum wage, a lot of people can't afford to pay for a *portera*. In many buildings intercom systems have been installed. (Here they are called *porteras electronicas*.) In time the traditional *portera* will disappear.

I've enjoyed my work. When I retire next year, I shall miss all my friends here.

I often wonder how I managed to cook in my tiny kitchen when there were nine of us living here.

The portera's *apartment: a place to call home.*

"Sports have been neglected in Spain"

Milagros Garcia Bonafé, 40, is a physical education teacher. She has spent most of her teaching career in her home town of Alcoy, but was recently transferred to a teacher training college in Madrid.

I began my career as a physical education teacher in 1962 in Alcoy, in the province of Alicante. The town has a population of 70,000 and I think it's typical of many medium-sized Spanish towns.

I was the first trained phys. ed. teacher to come to Alcoy. At the first two schools I worked in (one a state-run institute for secondary education and the other a church school) there were very few sports facilities. There was no gym or sports ground – just a big patio. Here, apart from doing phys. ed., pupils were able to play basketball, volleyball, and handball, which are the most common team games here. Soccer is the most important national sport at a professional level, but it is not so common in schools since most don't have playing fields. This doesn't mean that you won't find children playing soccer. You'll see them in any empty street or *plaza* (square) that they can find. Although the equipment supplied for phys. ed. has improved in the past twenty years (we now have vaulting-horses and mattresses), the patio is still the only place

we have to work on.

In contrast, another religious school I worked in, which was also in the town center, has been able to buy some land on the outskirts of the town. There they have built a magnificent sports center with a gym, five courts for basketball or netball and a large recreational area with a swimming pool.

But, in general, I would say that town planners hardly leave any *espacio verde* (park space) for sports activities. There are very few parks like the ones in the U.S. or England. But now the town councils are beginning to reclaim land to create recreational areas.

Skiing is another sport which has become popular here, but it's not easy to ski unless you live near the Pyrenees, La Sierra Nevada in Granada, or Navacerrada, close to Madrid. It also tends to be rather expensive.

Basically, the problem is that sports have been neglected in Spain. Only in the last few years have people (and politicians) begun to demand more facilities from the government. It is not just a question of building the sports facilities, but also of training more teachers and instructors. If you don't, you get a strange situation: the buildings are not fully used, because many people just don't know how to play a certain game.

The lack of qualified teachers is one of the problems that we are trying to overcome at the moment. I have recently been transferred to a teacher-training college in Madrid. We have 1,000 phys. ed. students. There is another center in Barcelona, but even so it is not enough. Training centers are planned for other cities. The only way to overcome the general ignorance about sports and phys. ed. is through schools. You can't expect the parents, who in many cases never had the chance to do any phys. ed. or sports themselves, to be able to teach their children.

The school patios have very few facilities for practicing sports.

A practical lesson in the gym at my training college.

"Life is hard – but I wouldn't change it"

Rafael Lamas, 45, is a fisherman in Galicia. He learned all about fishing from his father. The sea is in his blood. He would rather be a fisherman than anything else.

I'm an inshore fisherman, which means I go out in a small boat and fish near the coast. I live in a coastal village called Portonovo, where most people earn their living from the sea in one way or another. Galicia as a whole is famous for its fish and shellfish. In many of the *rias* (small estuaries) that are found all along the coast, there are mussel and clam farms.

My father used to go out every morning in his six-meter (20-ft) boat. It had a small triangular sail and oars. I began going out with him when I was eight. I learned all that I know about the sea from him.

On Sundays, when I normally don't go out fishing, I spend the morning repairing nets.

When he died, my father left me his boat and small house near the harbor. My brother and I decided that the best thing to do was to sell the house and land to one of the property developers. They had been in the village offering fairly good money for building land near the harbor. In this way, we were both able to break away from the life of poverty that fishermen traditionally lead. With the money we got from the sale of the house, my brother set up a small restaurant and I bought myself a new eleven-meter (36-ft) boat with a nice big engine. The boat is powerful enough to face up to any waves, wind or storm and get back to port safely. That's the only real difference between the way I fish and the way my father and grandfather did years ago. Thanks to a strong boat and a powerful engine, a fisherman is not risking his life every time he goes out, because here on the Atlantic coast we get some pretty nasty storms. I'm told that the Mediterranean is very temperamental as well. The weather is liable to change with alarming speed.

I carry a crew of two and every morning

Most of the people in Portonovo depend on the sea for their living.

we go out at dawn (weather permitting) to take in the nets and lobster pots that were set the previous evening. Our main catch is shellfish and octopus, but one of the problems we have is that the octopus, which might be as much as 1½ meters (5 feet) long including its tentacles, loves eating shellfish. If one of them gets into the lobster pot, we might find that it has eaten all the shellfish that had already been caught. This is a serious setback. Octopuses are very common and are sold cheaply, whereas we can get a much better price for lobsters, *centollos* (large crabs) and other shellfish.

After pulling in the nets at dawn, we immediately start back for port so we can put our catch on sale at the fish auction.

This system of selling fish hasn't changed at all over the years. But my father only used to have half a tub full of fish and shellfish to sell, and I come back with a catch that fills twelve to fifteen crates.

Whatever money I get for my catch is divided into three parts. One part goes to me as the boat owner, one part goes to the crew, and the third part is kept for the maintenance of the boat, nets and general fishing tackle.

Life as a fisherman is hard and I doubt if I will ever be rich, but I wouldn't change it for anything.

"I've paid for a meal with a painting!"

Isabel Grimalt Martinez, 38, is an artist in Sitges. She doesn't include herself among the painters who dream of fame, preferring the quiet life of a friendly village community.

I started working as an artist when I was 25, after separating from my husband. I had always enjoyed painting, but until then I had only painted as a hobby. Now I live entirely on what I can get from selling my paintings. It's not very much, but I prefer to live a quiet life in a village rather than get involved with art dealers and galleries in the big cities.

In Spain at the moment there must be at least 500 painters who are internationally recognized, at least in art circles. Spain has given birth to some great masters – Goya,

Perhaps the most curious paintings I do are the exvotos, or votive offerings.

Velazquez, and more recently, Pablo Picasso and Salvador Dali. You mustn't forget, either, that there are many artists who have still to achieve their greatest fame, such as Miró, Tapies, Saura, and Millares.

Perhaps it is because we have all these famous names as a part of our history and our present-day culture, that so many people hope to follow their example. I don't include myself among those painters who dream of fame and fortune. I have never given an exhibition of my paintings in an art gallery, although in Spain there are about 2,500 art galleries, which put on thousands of exhibitions each year. And that's without counting exhibitions that are organized in restaurants, shops and other places from time to time.

Apart from the 500 well-known artists, I think there must be about 10,000 painters like myself, who earn their living through painting. Many put on exhibitions. And many, like myself, take their paintings to one of the *plazas* (squares) in the city, where stalls are set up to sell directly to the public. It's part of Sunday morning routine

for people to go out for a stroll before lunch, and they like to wander around looking at the paintings. If I'm lucky they buy one from me. I usually paint watercolors, which I sell for about 1,500 pesetas ($11).

I live in a small seaside town where the pace of life is pretty slow, except when the tourists arrive in July and August. That's when I try to go away somewhere else. I enjoy the contact I have with the people of the town and most of us know each other. I find that the people in small towns like Sitges appreciate artists and welcome them into the community. More than once I've paid for meals with one of my paintings!

I like to go to the Placa del Pi in Barcelona, where I sell my paintings directly to the public.

Perhaps my favorite place for landscape painting is the island of Mallorca. On the northern coast there is some really spectacular scenery. It's mountainous and rugged, with sheer cliffs dropping 500 meters (1,640 ft) down to the sea below, and the pink and mauve hues of the rock contrast beautifully with the turquoise sea.

From time to time, I'm asked to do *exvotos* (votive offerings). These are religious paintings. They are used to give thanks to a saint or the Virgin Mary for having saved someone in danger. Traditionally, they were painted by sailors and often depicted a shipwreck.

"Barcelona is the capital for publishing in Castilian"

Ricardo Martin Tobias, 45, is Editorial Director of an important publishing house in Barcelona. He is also a professor of history at Barcelona University.

My first contact with printing and publishing dates back to when I was fifteen. I got a part-time job at a small printer's, cleaning the type and making it up to print. I started doing it to earn some pocket money, but the job soon began to mean much more to me than the money.

I'm lucky because Barcelona is a good place to learn about publishing. It is the world capital for publishing in Castilian. The market for our publications is not just limited to Spain, because of course Castilian is spoken in most of the countries in South America too. We also sell to the United States, where there are many Spanish-speaking citizens. In fact, Castilian is the third most important language in the world, if you base your judgement on the number of people who speak it.

So, there is a large market for the books we publish in Castilian, but this is not the case when we publish books in the other Spanish languages. Catalan, Basque and

Kioscos *are a typical sight in all Spanish towns and cities.*

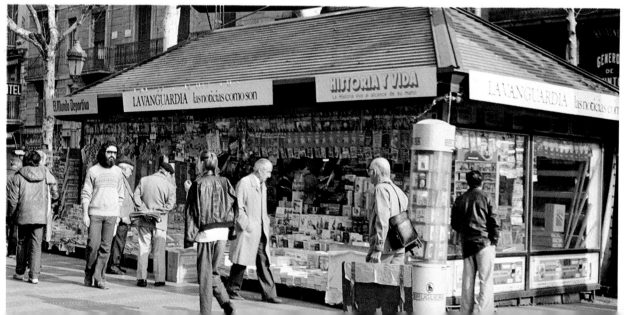

Two examples of our weekly magazines – the Encyclopedia of Decoration, *and one called* How does it work?

Galician are spoken by 5 to 10 million people in comparison with over 300 million who speak Castilian. This obviously makes publishing in minority languages more difficult from a business point of view. But efforts are being made to encourage these languages in all the arts, including books, theater, films and music.

I am the Editorial Director at one of the most important publishers in Spain. Most of our publications are encyclopedias. These are not big reference works, but small specialized encyclopedias, which are sold as weekly magazines. If you buy all the editions in a series, which may be as many as 120, you can have them bound into a single book. At the moment I am publishing the Encyclopedia of Decorating, which gives you all the know-how about interior decorating, using lots of photographs to illustrate the text.

This idea of publishing weekly magazines which can be compiled into a complete book is very popular these days. A big,
well-illustrated encyclopedia is very expensive, but if you buy a magazine every week for 100 pesetas (75 cents), you hardly notice the cost. The magazines are normally sold in the *kioscos* (newsstands), a typical sight in any Spanish town or city. These *kioscos* can be found on street corners, and more especially in the parts of the town where people like to go for a stroll, or sit out and have a drink. They don't sell just newspapers and magazines; many sell books as well.

Spain is not renowned as a country where people read a lot – either newspapers or books. But I think we are managing to increase our reading public by making our books attractive and easy to read, rather than just a collection of facts.

Apart from my work as an editor, I am also a professor at Barcelona University. There, my subjects are archaeology and the economic and social history of the ancient world. These days it's difficult to find time to do archaeological work. But I like to keep up to date with the latest discoveries and, whenever possible, I visit excavations either in South America or Europe.

Facts

Capital city: Madrid.

Principal language: Castilian Spanish is the official language. Catalan is widely spoken in the north-east, Basque in the north and Galician in the north-west.

Currency: One peseta = 100 centimos, and 136 pesetas are worth about one U.S. dollar (May 1983).

Religion: The established religion of the State is Roman Catholicism. Less than one percent of the population is Protestant, and there are also small numbers of Jews and Moslems.

Population: 37,538,200 (1980 estimate). The four main cities contain only about 17 percent of the population, with 65 percent living in the coastal areas. The interior provinces are thinly populated.

Climate: The Pyrenees maintain the prevailing dry conditions in Spain. Summers are hot, although in the hilly interior the winters are cold. The climate in the north is more temperate.

Government: Spain is a hereditary monarchy with the king as Head of State appointing the president of the government. Legislative power lies with the Cortes Generales (Parliament), which has two houses elected for four years by direct, universal, adult suffrage. The two houses are the Congress of Deputies, with 350 members elected by proportional representation; and the Senate, which has 248 members. Mainland Spain comprises 50 provinces, each having its own Council and Civil governor, as do the Balearic Islands. The Basque region is governed by the *Consejo General del Pais Vasco*, and Cataluña by the *Generalitat*.

Military service: Military service is compulsory and lasts for 18 months.

Education: Spain is divided into 12 educational districts, each with a university at its center. There are nursery schools (2–3 years); and kindergartens (4–5 years). Primary education, which is free, is compulsory from 6–14 years. Secondary education lasts 3 years (14–16 years) and leads to a *bachiller*. Pupils who do not go on to secondary education take compulsory first grade vocational training from 15 to 16 years. Potential university students take a one year "orientation" course, and entrance exams to the university are compulsory. There are 20 state universities as well as other autonomous and technical universities. Degree courses last 5 years and lead to a *licenciatura*. Student loans and subsidies for university fees are available from the government, but are minimal. In 1978 the study of Catalan in schools in Cataluña became compulsory.

Housing: The Ministry of Housing's policy is to create new cities or urban areas rather than undertake urban renewal projects. There are large-scale building projects to provide housing on credit for the poor.

Agriculture: Spain's economy relies partly on agriculture, with the most important industries involving the production of wine, sherry, and fruits. The main agricultural products are cereals, vegetables, fruit (mainly citrus), esparto-grass, hemp, flax, dried beans, olives, and cork. Wheat and cheap wines are giving way to meat, vegetables, and feed grains. The Government is promoting irrigation and the modernization of farming methods, because two-thirds of the country suffers from aridity. Other agricultural industries include silk (produced mostly in Murcia and Alicante) and the fisheries producing sardines, tuna fish and cod. Sheep and cattle rearing are also important.

Industry: Spain ranks tenth among the industrialized countries of the world; it is the fifth largest shipbuilder; the fourth largest wine-making country; one of the largest cement exporters; and the largest exporter of olive oil in the world. The car industry is the country's largest employer. Other important industries include the manufacture of cotton and woolen goods, chemical plants, machine tool and paper production. The heavy industries are concentrated in northern Spain. Tourism is very important – each year the number of tourists visiting Spain exceeds the entire indigenous population. Spain can satisfy local demand for most consumer goods. 1.4 million Spaniards were unemployed in 1981.

The Media: Most broadcasting is controlled by the *Direccion General de Radiofusion y Television*, although there are some privately-owned television stations, and a law permitting private television companies has been passed. *Radio Nacional Espanola* has home and foreign services. The home service consists of a national program, the second program (music), and the third program (culture), which all carry commercial advertising. *Television Espanola* broadcasts two channels. TV broadcasting is hindered by Spain's hilly topography. The Press in Spain consists of 167 daily newspapers, all printed in Castilian. The papers are published on a regional basis, so there are no national newspapers as such.

Index

Glossary

autonomy The right of self-government.

Basques People of unknown origin inhabiting the western Pyrenees in France and Spain.

castanets *(castañuelas)* Curved pieces of hollow wood, held between fingers and thumb and made to click together. Used especially by flamenco dancers.

Castilian The accepted standard form of Spanish language as spoken in Spain, based on the dialect of Spanish spoken in Castille.

Common Market Officially called the European Economic Community. An association composed of several European countries, which cooperate in matters of trade and economic policy.

Euskadi (The Basque Country) A region of northern Spain, with its own language and culture.

fascism A system of government (often ruled by a dictator) which controls everything in a country and which suppresses all public criticism or opposition.

General Franco Spanish military leader and dictator. After victory in the Civil War (1936–39), he established a dictatorship and ruled the country until his death in 1975.

Guardia Civil Spanish police force which looks after country areas, but is also responsible for policing ports, airports, frontiers and the coastline. It has a military structure.

lottery A game of chance in which tickets are sold to the public. A draw is made later, and the holder of that particular ticket wins a prize.

matador The bullfighter who kills the bull in a bullfight.

patron saint A saint regarded as the particular guardian of a country, church, trade or person.

socialism The belief that a country's industry, capital, land etc should belong to the community as a whole, not to private owners, and that the state should control and decide how these resources should be used.

Spanish Civil War The civil war in Spain 1936–39.

tenant farmer A person who farms land rented from another, the rent usually taking the form of part of the crops grown, or livestock reared.

town planning The planning of the physical and social development of a town.